Cute Bedtime Dog Picture Book Stories For Toddlers

Secrets Of A Puppy Series, Volume 1

Lenny Ford

Published by InfinitYou, 2017.

Copyright Notice
© Copyright 2017 InfinitYou

All rights reserved worldwide.

No part of this book can be reproduced or distributed in any way without written permission of the author.

Good Morning

I am the cute puppy, Lenny and I am just about to wake up in the room of my human sister Fanny.

I don't really know how I got in Fanny's room, because I have my own bed that is just for me.

I probably got scared during the night.

I guess, I had a bad dream and ran into Fanny's room to feel save and protected.

I am just a cute little puppy and still get scared a lot during the night.

I do not have lots of life experience yet, but one thing is for sure, I master the secrets of a cute puppy and this knowledge and skill is all I need to get me through the day without any trouble.

I will take you through one whole day of me and of my cute puppy life.

I will show you what it means to master the Secrets Of A Cute Puppy!

Welcome to my world and enjoy my story...The Secrets Of A Cute Puppy...

Breakfast

I am still confused but a big breakfast is going to make everything all right again.

I probably just got scared and must have had a bad dream during the night, so this is how I got in Fanny's room!

I am still confused about last night, but breakfast is more important for now and I start my breakfast with everything I like.

A hearty breakfast keeps body and mind together and today I am up for some fun!

Play Time

I got some helpful ideas from Tobby and Benny

After breakfast I am enjoying my play time with the two cats Tobby and Benny.

These two cats are so weird and so different from me.

Sometimes I wonder how they can keep up with their strange behaviour and independence.

I personally would hate to catch mice all day.

I love my human family and they love me and I feel our relationship is the best thing that ever happened to me.

The cats do not feel that way and go their own way without being much dependent on anybody.

Anyway, they got their way and I got mine, but in the end, we all love to play together and this is the thing that is most important to me.

Cookie Accident

Poor Mommy is cleaning up all the mess that I made.

Out of curiosity (I learned that from watching the cats), I jumped in the fishbowl where Mommy stocks all the yummie cookies.

Suddenly, all the cookies spilled over the glass. I hope she did not get too mad and I hope she does not tell anybody.

I guess, I must have done something wrong because the cats never get into trouble like this and they always do things so elegantly!

Sometimes I admire them for their artistic expertise.

I am more of the cute and clumsy kind and do things the opposite way.

My cute way of doing things is what sometimes helps me out, but in the fishbowl case, it really got me into trouble.

Heck, it almost destroyed Mommy's trust in me.

I hate to see that!

Next time, I have to watch the cats closer to discover their secret.

Is Mommy Mad?

Right after the cookie accident, I do not take any chances, so I prefer to wait outside for Mommy - like a cute puppy who knows how to behave well!

I really hope that she does not get too mad at me.

I guess once Mommy is done with cleaning up after me, she is going to take me for some grocery and bakery shopping.

I love these pastries!

She does take me every day and I hope today will not be different.

At The Bakery

The local bakery is my favorite place...

The bakery is my favorite place, but I have to stay outside.
   I am using the time wisely and watch the other puppies go by.
   Maybe I can make some friends to play with.

What Is For Lunch?

I love the kitchen time with Mommy.

Well, today she is not too sure about what is up for lunch.

She loves her family so much and tries to please everyone: Daddy, Kenny, Fanny, and Me!

I hope she is making my favorite bone.

She is the best cook I have ever met, because she is making the juiciest bone that I have ever tasted.

I Am Thinking Coookies

I am thinking apples, oranges, but I give all thumbs up for cookies.
    A juicy bone, cookies or a steak lunch are my all time favorites.
    I hope Mommy can read my mind.

Lunch Time

Finally at lunch time my dream comes to reality.

I finish lunch late with my human sister Fanny and my human brother Kenny who both came home very late from school today.

I wonder why?

I love to take all my time, because I enjoy my juicy bone for lunch so much.

Going To The Zoo

Jippie, I
 don't get punished for the early morning cookie accident, but we all do something fun together.
 We are going to the Zoo.
 What a surprise for the afternoon.
 I love the Zoo, because I love exotic animals.

At The Zoo

I am so fascinated with all the exotic animals from the Zoo.

I love watching the variety of animals at the Zoo.

They are all looking very different to each other.

The giraffe is the tallest animal. The elephant is the loudest animal and needs lots of water to be happy.

The snake is the most dangerous animal. The monkey is the most funny animal.

I am very scared of the lion and do not hope to meet him alone at night.

So my question to you: "Who is cuter, the animals at the Zoo or me?"

Reflexions In The Park

Coming back from the Zoo with Mommy, Daddy, Kenny, and Fanny, I have some time to think about the animals from the Zoo.

I enjoy our walk back home. We are taking a shortcut through the Park and are still intoxicated from the Zoo
animals.

We were able to watch the lion, the elephants, the giraffe, the crocodiles, the funny monkeys and the hippopotamus.

I am a fun spirit myself and love watching the monkeys most, because they remind me of humans but in a fun way!

I feel that from watching the monkeys a lot, I can learn a lot about humans - and this is what I am after.

I love to please the humans and am very keen on learning how to get along with them in the best way.

I know that once I am going to be a very behaved cute little puppy, Mommy and my whole human family will love me even more.

I love the Zoo, because I am learning so much from it and a wise puppy is a cute puppy!

Playing In The Backyard

I love playing with my puppy buddies in the backyard, but today my precious little fur is getting really dirty from the mud outside.

There is no rain in sight at all so that the rain might help me getting cleaned up.

Hopefully Mommy is going to make me a nice hot bath afterwards.

These games are fun and addictive and there is only one thing that is better than playing with my friends:

Steak dinners, World Peace, some decent quality fur and hair products to keep my looks up and Cookies!

I Love The Bathtub

Mommy in her bathtub and me in mine.

Look how Mommy is taking care of my delicate fur and how she is grooming me with real good care!

She even brushes my teeth so that I smell extra fresh.

Before And After

Look at my before and after pictures.
    I was really dirty from play time and needed a nice hot bath and Mommy hers.
    I feel really clean and groomed now and I totally enjoyed that relaxing bath with Mommy.

Playtime With Mommy

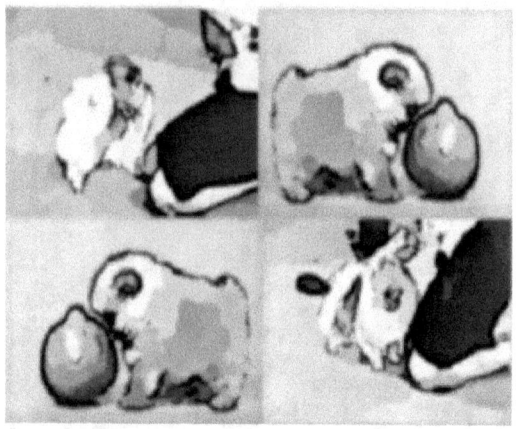

Oh, that bath was wonderful and now it is time for Mommy and me to get ready and dressed up for dinner.

She loves to brush and groom me and make me beautiful for dinner time.

I really love my Mommy and remember that I have to be a better puppy tomorrow so that my Mommy will love me as much as I love her.

I just want her to be very proud of me!

Oh, I am suddenly feeling a bit hungry before dinner because play time and bath time has been taking a lot of energy from me.

Mommy always gives me a treat before dinner when I am good.

Today I am very good and she seems to remember her rule for my treat.

Today she gives me an extra big treat and I guess this means that she really does love me and probably she is extra proud of me, today!

If she is happy, I am double time happy.

I know that I am not doing too much to make her happy these days, but, heck, the Secrets Of A Cute Puppy still kind of work on her!

Dinner Time

A big night for me because we are all having dinner together.

See how beautiful my Mommy has made herself for Daddy.

I am enjoying the whole atmospere with candles and happy family members.

The only problem I am having right now is that I am not really hungry.

I wonder why?

Probably it has something to do with my treat that I got from Mommy before dinner.

I hope she does not find out.

Quality TV Time

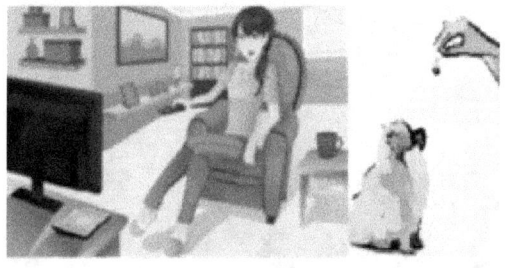

I always enjoy some quality TV time with Mommy after dinner.

We are able to watch some quality movies while the boys are watching a game in the other room and little Fanny is already sleeping in her room.

Everything is really peaceful and quiet this time of the day and I am enjoying the placid atmosphere in the cosy room with Mommy.

Around midnight when the last movie ends is the time when I am getting hungry again.

This is the time when I can't help thinking about the juiciest bone ever!

Nobody in my family seems to care for anything to eat right now, because they all enjoyed their dinner, except me!

I guess having a treat right before dinner is not such a brilliant idea at all!

Before Bedtime

Now it is time to think about bedtime and finally my dream comes true.
    Yes, I am getting a nice treat from Mommy.
    But guess what!
    Mommy does not seem to care about my juicy bone dream and she only gives me a small treat (not even in the slightest way in the shape of a bone!), while I am still hungry.
    This is not my dream come true at all.
    This is rather a very unpleasant and unsatisfying moment for me.

I Hate Everything

I hate everything and I am still hungry because the treat before bedtime was much too small.

By now, I have already decided that I will not accept any treat before dinner anymore.

I am serious about this, because I want to enjoy my dinner like the adults do.

Sometimes we cute puppies do not have an easy time with these grown ups.

They sometimes treat us at the very wrong moment.

Time To Think

Not only that I am still hungry, but I am having lots of mental trouble these days.

Soon school starts for me and the fun days with Mommy at home and at the Park are over!

With these scary thoughts I am falling asleep and I am trying to picture my new life as a cute puppy at school.

Tomorrow Will Be Another Day

I still hate everything, because I am still hungry, grrrrhhh, but there is not much I can do about it.

There is only one thing that keeps me calm and positive.

Tomorrow will be another day and everything will be better.

Yes, I'll think about my troubles tomorrow with a clear head and deep in my heart I do know that no matter how hopeless and bad my problems might look now, there is another day coming tomorrow.

Yes, that kind of thinking is the solution!

Tomorrow will be another day and I am going to be a cuter puppy and do everything correctly and properly so that Mommy is going to love me forever.

This also includes not accepting any treat before dinner (under any circumstance!) because sometimes we cute puppies have to educate the human race.

Conclusion

Yes, these are truly the Secrets Of A Cute Puppy and if you have a cute puppy at home, listen to your puppy carefully, because sometimes you can learn a lot from your puppy.

Yes, your puppy is indeed teaching you very wise and valuable lessons.

Just listen and observe your puppy in a smart way.

Listening to your puppy and observing your puppy will help you find out the most secretly guarded things that you might not even have known about your puppy.

These are the true "Secrets Of A Cute Puppy!"

Your puppy will reveal them to you once you are ready for them.

That's it for now and until the next time have a very fun and exciting time with your cute puppy that you have at home, or maybe you get one soon.

See you around in my next cute puppy story!

With Love,
    Lenny

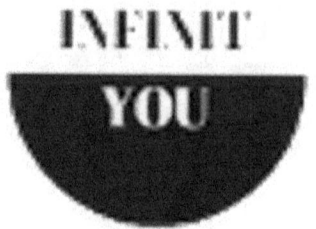

About the Publisher

InfinitYou is a hybrid general interest trade publisher. One of the first of its kind InfinitYou publishes physical books, electronic books, and audiobooks in various genres. Our publications are meant to educate, edify and entertain readers of all walks of life from babies to the elderly. Home to more than twenty imprints such as Infinit Baby, Infinit Kids, Infinit Girl, Infinit Boy, Infinit Coloring, Infinit Swear Words, Infinit Activities, Infinit Productivity, Infinit Cat, Infinit Dog, Infinit Love, Infinit Family, Infinit Survival, Infinit Health, Infinit Beauty, Infinit Spirituality, Infinit Lifestyle, Infinit Wealth, Infinit Romance, and lots more.

www.ingramcontent.com/pod-product-compliance
Lightning Source LLC
LaVergne TN
LVHW020740090526
838202LV00057BA/6141